PAGES OF THE WOUND

John Berger

PAGES OF THE WOUND

Poems drawings photographs 1956-96

BLOOMSBURY
CIRCLE PRESS

First published by John Christie at Circle Press, 1994
(ISBN 0 901380 695)

This paperback edition published 1996

Bloomsbury Publishing Plc, 38 Soho Square, London W1V 5DF

'At Remaurian' was first published as a small inset
book in Typographica 11 (1965).

A CIP catalogue record for this book
is available from the British Library

ISBN 0 7475 2975 2

Printed in Great Britain by Lawrence - Allen, Weston- super-Mare

Pages of the Wound is the result of a collaboration between John Christie, who printed the original book, and myself. Earlier we collaborated in making four films together. Without his faith and above all his vision and care, the book would never have acquired the form it has. On this page quite simply I want to thank him for his friendship. J.B.

Opposite page: 'Self-portrait' 1945 (from an etching, plate lost)

Since the age of twelve I have written poems when I could do nothing else. Poems are born of a sense of helplessness – hence their force.

Writing a poem is the opposite of riding a motor bike. Riding, you negotiate at high speed around every fact you meet. Body and machine follow your eyes which find their way through, untouched. Your sense of freedom comes from the fact that the wait between decision and consequence is minimal, and what resistance or delay there is, you use as ricochet. When riding, if you want to go on living, you think of nothing else but what is there.

Poems are helpless before the facts. Helpless but not without endurance, for everything resists them. They find names for the consequences, not for the decisions.

Writing a poem you listen to everything save what is happening now. Like the dress, the shoes kicked off and the hairbrush, they speak of what is not there. Or, rather, of what is not there in front of you.

From around the Galician town of Betanzos in north-west Spain, thousands of emigrants a century ago left for Florida, Cuba and Central America. And so, for them, Betanzos, the name, became interiorised. This is why on drawing after drawing I have written that word.

On a bike the rider weaves through, and poems head in the opposite direction. Yet shared sometimes between the two, as they pass, there is the same pity of it. And in that, my love, the same love . . .

Far Away

Was it my father
who laid this wood?

Is the hand
that strikes the match
        historic?

The wind cross-questioned
and the tongues of flame
replied.

The emigrant's fire.

On my knees
to balance the saucepan
kitchen mother
kerchief head
I recall you
and call you again.

The poppies of your yard
are scattered in my clouds.

1975/76

Born. 5/11/26

Redder every day
the leaves of the pear trees.
Tell me what is bleeding.
Not summer
for summer left early.
Not the village
for the village though drunk on its road
has not fallen.
Not my heart
for my heart bleeds no more
than the arnica flower.

Nobody has died this month
or been fortunate enough
to receive a foreign work-permit.
We fed with soup
let sleep in the barn
no more thoughts of suicide
than is normal in November.
Tell me what is bleeding
you who see in the dark.

Hands of the world
amputated by profit
bleed in
streets of bloodsheds.

1983

Rural Emigration

Mornings were mothers
bringing up their pastures
drying invisible sheets
across the orchard
and teasing the steaming rocks
with tales of sun and bed.

The evenings planted fences
watched the poultry
peck in the dog-high grass
gathered their bragging clouds
and thundered passion
to the feeding mothers.

Day after day
morning and evening coupled
grass and leaves grew up
and the drenched green catkins
fell from our walnut tree
like dead caterpillars.

1979

Leavings

Brightest guests have gone
Green furnishings are down,
Shadeless light condones
Black frost on window panes.

Where lovers and grasses
Spent their seeds
Over iron crevices
Ice now makes the beds.

Yet indulge no regret.
Mouse eye of robin,
Creeping silence,
These cautious lines,

Bear witness still
In their circumvention
To the constant
Tenancy of man.

1956/57

Ypres

Base: fields whose mud is waterlogged

Perpendicular: thin larches
                planted in rows
                    with broken
                        branches

Horizontal: brick walls the colour of
                dead horses

Sinking: lower
            and lower
                houses with dark windows

Sometimes a wall is white-washed
a rectangle of dead lime
            under the indifferent clouds

Here all poultry should have webbed feet
At dusk drowned soldiers cross the fields to steal chickens

Through base
            perpendicular
            and horizontal
                there is order:
                the order of split wood
                broken branches
                walls the colour of dead horses
                and roofs fallen in

There is no way out except across
Nothing reaches any heaven from here

Between earth and sky there is
            a transparent canopy
            plaited from cock crows
            and the cries of soldiers

1973

Self-portrait 1914-18

It seems now that I was so near to that war.
I was born eight years after it ended
When the General Strike had been defeated.

Yet I was born by Very Light and shrapnel
On duck boards
Among limbs without bodies.

I was born of the look of the dead
Swaddled in mustard gas
And fed in a dugout.

I was the groundless hope of survival
With mud between finger and thumb
Born near Abbeville.

I lived the first year of my life
Between the leaves of a pocket bible
Stuffed in a khaki haversack.

I lived the second year of my life
With three photos of a woman
Kept in a standard issue army paybook.

In the third year of my life
At 11am on November 11th 1918
I became all that was conceivable.

Before I could see
Before I could cry out
Before I could go hungry

I was the world fit for heroes to live in.

1970

Words I

for Beverly

Down the gorge
        ran
                people and blood

In the bracken
        beyond touch
                a dog howled

A head between lips
        opened
                the mouth of the world

Her breasts
        like doves
                perch on her ribs

Her child sucks the long
        white thread
                of words to come

Words II

The tongue
        is the spine's first leaf
forests of language surround it

Like a mole
        the tongue
burrows through the earth of speech

Like a bird
        the tongue
flies in arcs of the written word

The tongue is tethered and alone in its mouth

1980

Brain-Storm

in the centre
of the dried cloves
which form the brain
of the garlic
thrown in the bowl
of oddments in
the basement kitchen
of the suburban home
a premonition of green
ferociously proposes
the sun's prodigal return.

1982

A Dream Which I Inscribed Verbatim

Not the horse run wild
nor the men on their feet dismounted
could lead her through the wood to believe
            that he had truly died.

O bite the lobe of his ear, they said,
and draw the bolt of his life.

There at the end of the green leafed ride
they hanged him on a holly holly tree
and she wept 'til her tears rolled stones
            down my mountain side.

1960

Postcard From Troy

In this metropolis
death wears a sheep skin

along the freeways
the traffic never stops

beneath the side street waterfall
three coffins full

baa baa black sheep

grass grows in the taxis

who can reverse
the hour glass of gravel?

to pin down
the wall to wall carpet
wood anemones are hammered in

yes sir yes sir
the gate is shut

only enough to wrap
dead bunting in.

1990

Rembrandt Self-portrait

The eyes from the face
two nights look at the day
the universe of his mind
doubled by pity
nothing else can suffice.
Before a mirror
silent as a horseless road
he envisaged us
deaf dumb
returning overland
to look at him
in the dark.

1975

Poetry

Word by word I describe
you accept each fact
and ask yourself:
what does he really mean?

Quarto after quarto of sky
salt sky
sky of the placid tear
printed from the other sky
punched with stars.
Pages laid out to dry.

Birds like letters fly away
O let us fly away
circle and settle on the water
near the fort of the illegible.

1972   *Les Salins de Giraud*

For Howe 1909 –1985

I know you
by my ignorance
and its space
which shyly
you filled with quotations

I know you
by the half smile of your reticence
and the space
of a pride
you hid in patched sleeves

I know you
by the moment before death
and the space
of God
you found in the lament of words

I know you
by your daughter
and the space
of the words
between here and then

18.7.85

AT REMAURIAN

for Sven, Romaine and Anya

1.

Down from the mountain
The yellow of knife-handles
Past the olives
To the age of my mill
Wherein stone pacifies stone
With the oil of season after season
And a man sleeping
May be woken
By the stillness of my wheel.

2.

A butterfly disturbs a grain
The grain another
Till there is such friction in the dust
The sky spills its blue milk
On the stones that have conceived

A day is born

Down the precipitous gaze of its opened eyes
The trees are led.

3.

At the nocturnal level of the hand
Herbs must always grow
Leaf of my leaf
But early enough
And upright
Following in the wake of the trees
I have felt against the vein of my wrist
Webs breaking
Till every connection of the night is severed
And single I step forward to become
The honey-coloured fleck
On the iris of the first comer's eye.

AT REMAURIAN

4.

Seen naked the day rises
Till its eye can probe
Beyond walls on which lizards tattooed
Beat the rate of my pulse
Through groves so ancient
No desire of mine
Can be separate from its origin
In the glance of a man
A millennium ago
Down erogenous slopes
Where poised boulders await
The staring
Behind a cataract of pleasure
Over hills patient as the unconceived
To that horizon
Which miles moisten in their welcome
And sight divides.

5.

Let the drawing stand up
And every dot
Yield a line
As the field that was sown
Is raised by its crop
And my nipple by the slow-growing tree

Let the drawing stand up
And make of my legs
The legs of the table
On which this land is
Laid out like a towel
And placed like a bowl
Awaiting its water

Let the drawing stand up
And its weight bear down
Till every line is opened
And the distance they cover
Is the format of the sky
Above my lover

Let the drawing stand up
And pour from its lip
All that can turn my wheel.

6.

As I climb
The mountain sweats

The heart beats faster
Stones drip
To trickle down the spine

In the valley
The mouth of the river like a rumour
Whispers water in the ear of the fields

Before it is dark
From this summit my mountain
You must descend me.

7.

Cover me cover me
That I am spread as the whiteness of rock
And no ignorance remains in the light
When every organ
With its workings is displayed
Letting spermatozoa and egg
Be as evident to sight
As pairing butterflies
The glance of whose wings
It will then be too late
For this gazing sun
Ever to misinterpret.

8.

Sweet clamour
And the voice of a child
In the torrent of my cries
Helped you name
The unnameable colour
Of my womb
Since from your bough
My leaves then unfolded
And I pursued
With my tongue
The lineage of your wood.

AT REMAURIAN

9.

Stones still warm
Taste of your hands

Length and height lose
Their terraced scale

The light descends to the level sea
With the waters of the robe I do not wear

The dark examines us
By touch alone.

1962/63

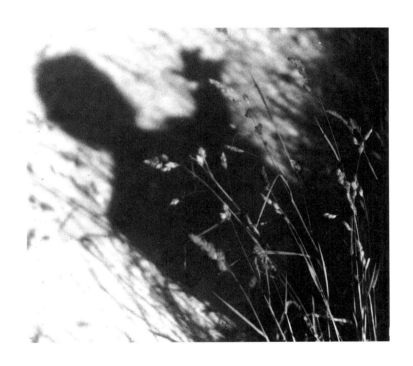

Mortality

each second
a leaf falls in the forest of my head
whilst
those who say they love me
hunt a wild boar
believing it
has savaged me

1970

Migrant Words

In a pocket of earth
I buried all the accents
of my mother tongue

there they lie
like needles of pine
assembled by ants

one day the stumbling cry
of another wanderer
may set them alight

then warm and comforted
he will hear all night
the truth as lullaby

1980

Music

The canary sings inside the eagle
and is mad.
The canary sings inside the cage
of the eagle's breast.
The slow beat of the eagle's wings
accelerated
flows like an incessant giggle
musically
from the canary's quivering beak.
The canary trills highest
when the eagle kills.

1972

Elvis

The black bird in the
birch tree
exchanges his wings
for leaves
sings
to the wisteria
and disappears
for ever
into the foliage of
applause.

1991

Two Poems of the Taiga

for Nella

1.

Perhaps our sledge is made of its speed
your outstretched hand our blanket
a foreign language learnt at night
      the track we take
         between the trees.

You have filled the thermos with coffee
packed our footprints if needed
to throw into the jaws
      of the untestifying
         ravenous snow.

Together like carpenters with hammers
we have taught the distance
how to build a roof
      from the trees
         we fly between.

In the silence left behind
I no longer hear the far away
question of the summer house:
      and tomorrow
         where shall we go?

At dusk the harnessed dogs fear
there's no end to the forest
and in the snow every night
      we calm them
         with our surprising laughter.

2.

In the undergrowth
      light is a hammered nail
in the undergrowth
      words are spoken by the dead
in the undergrowth
      the news is of prison
knowing the worst
      the undergrowth chose us.

In the undergrowth
      from wild boars we learnt tact
in the undergrowth
      we read the frost of stars
carrying the undergrowth
      we heated ovens for bread
knowing the worse
      we chose the undergrowth.

You from the plain
      I from the sea
we recalled horizons.
      Or did we foresee them
in the undergrowth
      where you and I slept
in each other's arms
      like forsaken skies?

1980

Kerchief

In the morning
folded with its wild flowers
washed and ironed
it takes up little space in the drawer.

Shaking it open
she ties it round her head.

In the evening she pulls it off
and lets it fall
still knotted to the floor.

On a cotton scarf
among printed flowers
a working day
has written its dream.

1981

Maritsa Plain

The agronomists in pointed shoes
step over the dead dog
dragged to the border of the highway
entering the field they bend
to examine handfuls of black soil
the wind furls their lightweight suits
around their limbs
like the air from a gigantic experimental fan
and the peasants
in their patches and quilted jackets
look on and ask:
what in our familiar earth
can they hope to find?

1978

Road 1

EIGHT POEMS OF EMIGRATION

1. Village

I tell you
        all houses
are holes in an arse of stone

we eat off coffin lids

between evening star
        and milk in a bucket
is nothing

the churn is emptied
        twice a day

cast us
        steaming
                on the fields.

2. Earth

the purple scalp of the earth
combed in autumn
        and times of famine

the metal bones of the earth
        extracted by hand

the church above the earth
        arms of our clock crucified

all is taken.

3. Leaving

pain
cannot

endure long enough

tracks vanish
under snow
the white embrace
of leaving

I have tried to write the truth on trains

without an ear
the tongue takes fright
clings to a single word
the train is crossing a bridge
black ice collects
on each letter
S A V A
my river

4.   Metropolis

the edge of moonlight
sharp
like the level
        of water in a canal

and the locks of reason
at dawn
when the level of the dark
is brought down
        to that of the light

accept the dark
massed black
zone of blindness
accept it eyes

but here the dark
has been stolen in a sack
weighted down with a pebble
and drowned

there is no longer any dark.

5.   Factory

here
it is dawn eternally
hour of awakening
hour of revolutionary prophecy
hour of the embers dead
time of the days work
without end

there we built the night
as we lit the fire
lay down in it
pulled up the dark as blanket

near fields were
the breath of animals asleep
quiet as the earth
warm as the fire

cold is the pain of believing
warmth will never return

here
night is time forgotten
eternal dawn
and in the cold I dream
        of how the pine
        burnt
        like a dog's tongue
        behind its teeth.

6. Waterfront

all night Hudson
coughs in bed

I try to sleep

my country
is a hide nailed to wood

the wind of my soul rushes

out of horizons
I make a hammock

in sleep
I suck birth village
touch my river's curve

two black mackerel
pilot in
daybreak

gaff them sky gaff them

7. Absence

when the sun was no higher than the grass
jewels hung in the trees
and the terraces turned rose
between fluorescent lights along the ringroad
apartments hang their pietas

they are frying potatoes
a factory discharges its hands in woollen gloves
there is a hole in my thumb

the vines are not green
the vines are not here
the jewels
crushed in high voltage wires
will be worn by the dead
DANGER DE MORT.

8.   A Forest I Knew

let me die like this

the branches have muscles
        hills get up
the cloud pours
        into a cup

in the forest wild boar
        have eaten
        are warm
                and sleepy

each clearing is recorded
        on a screen I carry
rolled like a cloth
        in my head

a sheet
        pulled over
                the eyes of the dead
keeps out the look of the world
on the cloth
        unrolled
I follow their spoor
        in the forest I knew.

1984

Solitary Shepherd's Moonrise

On that horizon
engraved on each day
like the crack in the coffee bowl
cows become the size they were
when I was four

To the north of the cows
graze the rocks
named the Tall Ones
there where the moon rises
when all has been done

First a pink halo
the colour of the dress
worn at a dance by her
father my father they say
went barefoot for

The dress has no hem my son

Then a lake of pale skin
there where the sons swam
one last night
and the boots they left on the bank
never to climb again

The horizon opens like a mouth my son

Slowly slowly
the bone white head is born
your body of light
slips trailing out
from where my god you came.

1980

Distant Village

The mountains are pitiless
the rain is melting the snow
it will freeze again.

In the cafe two strangers
play the accordion
and the roomful of men are singing.

Tunes are filling
the sacks of the heart
the troughs of eyes.

Words are filling
the stalls
which bellow between the ears.

Music shaves the jowls
loosens the joints,
the only cure for rheumatism.

Music cleans the nails
softens our hands
scours the callouses.

A roomful of men
come from drenched cattle,
diesel oil, the eternal shovel,

are caressing
the air of a love song
with sweetened hands.

Mine have left my wrists
and are crossing the mountains
to find your breasts.

In the cafe two strangers
play the accordion
the rain is melting the snow.

1986

16.45h   The Firing Squad

The dog carried the day
in her mouth
over the fields of the small hours
towards a hiding place
which before had been safe.

Nobody was woken before dawn.

At noon
the dog sprawling in the shade
placed the pup between her four paws
and waited in vain
for it to suck.

A line of prisoners
hands knotted
fall forward
into the grave they have dug.

Belly to the earth
the dog carries the day
which has never stirred
back to its dark.

Under the stars the bereaved
imagine they hear
a dog howling too
on the edge of the world.

This piteous day was born
stone-deaf and blind.

1991

Separation

We with our vagrant language
we with our incorrigible accents
and another word for milk
we who come by train
and embrace on platforms
we and our wagons
we whose voice in our absence
is framed on a bedroom wall
we who share everything
and nothing –
this nothing which we break in two
and wash down with a gulp
from the only bottle,
we whom the cuckoo
taught to count,
into what currency
have they changed our singing?
What in our single beds
do we know of poetry?

We are experts in presents
both wrapped ones
and the others left surreptitiously.
Before leaving we hide our eyes our feet our backs.
What we take is for the luggage rack.
We leave our eyes behind
in the window frames and mirrors
we leave our feet behind
on the carpet by the bed
we leave our backs behind
in the mortar of the walls
and the doors hung on their hinges.

The door closed behind us
and the noise of the wagon wheels.

We are experts too in taking.
We take with us anniversaries
the shape of a fingernail
the silence of the child asleep
the taste of your celery
and your word for milk.

What in our single beds
do we know of poetry?

Single track, junction and
marshalling yards
read out loud to us.
No poem has longer lines
than those we have taken.
Like horsedealers we know how
to look a distance in the mouth
and judge its pain by its teeth.

With mules, on foot
by airliners and lorries
in our hearts
we carry everything,
harvests, coffins, water,
oil, hydrogen, roads,
flowering lilac and
the earth thrown into the mass grave.

We with our bad foreign news
and another word for milk
what in our single beds
do we know of poetry?

We know as well as the midwives
how women carry children
and give birth,
we know as well as the scholars
what makes a language quiver.

Our freight.
The bringing together of what has been parted
makes a language quiver.
Across millennia and the village street
through tundra and forests
by farewells and bridges
towards the city of our child
everything must be carried.

We carry poetry
as the cattle trucks of the world
carry cattle.
Soon in the sidings
they will sluice them down.

1985

Road 2

We ta
the sh
the
the tos
and

Requiem

Green
fills
the earth's two breasts
day and night
trees of the forest
suckle green.
Of all the colours
green is the last.

Wind
dries the soil
powdery and light
in the deepest clay
stains
the brown of blood
repeatedly dried
die again
as the wind drops
under the rain.

Green
unlike silver or red
I say to you Nella
is never still
green who waited
mineral ages
for the leaf
is the colour of their souls
and comes as gift.

1986

Twelve Theses on the Economy of the Dead

1. The dead surround the living. The living are the core
    of the dead. In this core are the dimensions of time and
    space. What surrounds the core is timelessness.

2. Between the core and its surroundings there are
    exchanges, which are not usually clear. All religions
    have been concerned with making them clearer.
    The credibility of religion depends upon the clarity of
    certain unusual exchanges. The mystifications of
    religion are the result of trying to systematically produce
    such exchanges.

3. The rarity of clear exchange is due to the rarity of what
    can cross intact the frontier between timelessness
    and time.

4. To see the dead as the individuals they once were tends
    to obscure their nature. Try to consider the living as we
    might assume the dead to do: collectively.
    The collective would accrue not only across space but
    also throughout time. It would include all those who
    had ever lived. And so we would also be thinking of the
    dead. The living reduce the dead to those who have
    lived; yet the dead already include the living in their
    own great collective.

5. The dead inhabit a timeless moment of construction
    continually rebegun. The construction is the state
    of the universe at any instant.

6. According to their memory of life, the dead know the
    moment of construction as, also, a moment of collapse.
    Having lived, the dead can never be inert.

7.   If the dead live in a timeless moment, how can they have a memory? They remember no more than being thrown into time, as does everything which existed or exists.

8.   The difference between the dead and the unborn is that the dead have this memory. As the number of dead increase, the memory enlarges.

9.   The memory of the dead existing in timelessness may be thought of as a form of imagination concerning the possible. This imagination is close to (resides in) God; but I do not know how.

10. In the world of the living there is an equivalent but contrary phenomenon. The living sometimes experience timelessness, as revealed in sleep, ecstasy, instants of extreme danger, orgasm, and perhaps in the experience of dying itself. During these instants the living imagination covers the entire field of experience and overruns the contours of the individual life or death. It touches the waiting imagination of the dead.

11. What is the relation of the dead to what has not yet happened, to the future? All the future *is* the construction in which their 'imagination' is engaged.

12. How do the living live with the dead? Until the dehumanisation of society by capitalism, all the living awaited the experience of the dead. It was their ultimate future. By themselves the living were incomplete. Thus living and dead were inter-dependent. Always. Only a uniquely modern form of egotism has broken this inter-dependence. With disastrous results for the living, who now think of the dead as the *eliminated*.

1994

Alpine Spring 1993

The scythe cuts
the windows of that house are lit
the first grass
who is missing this night?
the swallows arrive
the topmost branches of the plum trees
all are missing
are points of needles' eyes
accupunctures of blossom
a thousand kilometres south in that house
the wounded have no anaesthetics
the swallows go
and men prepare to die
between the telephone wires
the spring grass falls
the windows are black
we should mourn
there should be many plums this year
the new leaves
towns besieged
tiny as the darling fingernails
of a baby whose mother has been raped then shot
accupunctures of white blossom
and the wooden planks of the barn
where the swallows nest
the same wood as the cross
I'm scything the spring grass
on which Christ dies
amidst sunlit blossoms agape
at the blue sky.

Toussaint
for Nelia

The aunt is feeding the hens
and I'm her chick

The aunt is scrubbing the floor
and I'm her sunlight

The aunt is podding peas
and I'm her pinch of sugar

The aunt is making jam
and I'm her jam-jar cover

The aunt's asleep on her back
and I'm her future

And on All Soul's Day now
how I miss her

1993

Robert Jorat

This morning Robert
I polished my black boots
to be correct and neat
for your adieu

Your coffin was small
and one of your granddaughters
lit the candles
for its four corners

You taught me
the dying art
of sharpening a scythe
with a hammer

At your grave side
I see your thumb nail
testing the blade
thin as foil

With the years you grew frailer
and I tapped
to draw the steel
each year thinner

Yet afterwards
you always took the blade
and with a short hammer
corrected my ineptitudes

Next June
I must sharpen the scythe alone
and for you I will try Robert
to make it sharper than my grief

1996

Mostar
for Simon and Lilo

On the Saturday mornings
reduced to dust
on the Saturday mornings
of weeks
which had seven normal days
and seven quiet nights –
unless we drank
on Saturday mornings I'd
carry out to the balcony
my shoes
and a pair or two of hers –
she had fourteen pairs
on the fifth floor
among the pigeons
my finger in a scrap of rag
circling the tip of polish
balanced on the balustrade
I applied the black
to the little sides
the snub toe
the slender heel
whose tip was no larger than a dice
for her right foot and left
then I'd leave them a moment
saying to myself
it does good
to let the wax feed the leather
before taking the brush
and with two fingers poked in the toe
polishing them
til they shone
on Saturday morning.

The brush
the fifth floor
the feet
All has vanished.
1995

Song

your tongue
        long as a snake's
and not forked

your leaning neck
        where they planted
a single tree

your skin ocean
        glistening drop
and kingdom

our four eyes
        a knotted black silk
for the blind

who'll lead us
        laughing to the seed
of what we were

1996